T0198776

Highly SENSITIVE

A Story About An Empath's Journey To Freedom

Julie Klutinoty

Balboa Press books may be ordered through booksellers or by contacting:

Balboa Press
A Division of Hay House
1663 Liberty Drive
Bloomington, IN 47403
www.balboapress.com
844-682-1282

Because of the dynamic nature of the Internet, any web addresses or links contained in this book may have changed since publication and may no longer be valid. The views expressed in this work are solely those of the author and do not necessarily reflect the views of the publisher, and the publisher hereby disclaims any responsibility for them.

Any people depicted in stock imagery provided by Getty Images are models, and such images are being used for illustrative purposes only.
Certain stock imagery © Getty Images.

Interior Image Credit: Julie Klutinoty

ISBN: 979-8-7652-3428-0 (sc)
ISBN: 979-8-7652-3429-7 (e)

Library of Congress Control Number: 2022916712

Print information available on the last page.

Balboa Press rev. date: 09/22/2022

Highly SENSITIVE

A Story About An Empath's Journey To Freedom

CONTENTS

Forward by Julie Klutinoty

While this book, Highly Sensitive, merely touches on the aspects of living as a Highly Sensitive Empath, there is depth to each chapter.

I invite you to take your time when reading this book, as the pictures and the words are very much contributing to your journey forward. Allow yourself to reflect and ponder your own experiences and how you perceive the world. How you 'feel' the world and those around you. It wasn't until I began teaching workshops and socializing with other Empaths that I truly saw what a remarkable gift being Highly Sensitive is.

I wish you many, many peaceful blessings on your path inward to accepting and appreciating who you are and becoming to know how *special* you are.

Love,
Julie

CHAPTER 1

Being Highly Sensitive

If you are reading this book and you know you are *'Highly Sensitive'*, Congratulations! There is nothing wrong with you. You *are* divinely guided and protected at all times.

Regardless of how you came into awareness of your beautiful Empathic Gifts, you have been blessed with the ability to sense and feel what others do not. For this reason, know that you are indeed, *special*. You are different from those who are less sensitive and you have different needs.

This book is about my journey, as an Empath, into the realization of exactly how different I was than the rest of my family, especially growing up. For me, it has been a journey into my own understanding through personal experiences of what being 'highly sensitive' means and how it can effect how I live my life. It has also been a realization of how different my needs are from many of those around me.

Wherever you may be on your own self realization journey, remember, 'There Is Nothing Wrong With You!' You are Love and you are Light and most often than not, if you are highly sensitive, you are being effected or impacted by the energy and those around you. This book is a story about an Empath finding her Freedom!

My intention is not to stay in 'story' but to extract the gifts of my experiences and when applicable, share the experience in the context which it occurred. For me, this is where the 'medicine' lies and where healing can take place. Regardless of the experience or the lesson, if you are not wanting to heal, learn or let go - there is a potential for suffering.

We all have a choice. Do you intend to live 'God's Will' or do you intend to live by 'Free Will and Choice'? Living **God's Will** means you are able to bypass your egoic mind and live from your heart as a heart centered Being, coming from a place of 'oneness', connecting to your Higher Self. It is a community minded way of Being.

The other, living **Free Will and Choice** refers to the actions, wants and desires in your life as coming from the man - made thinking mind, the *little ego*. This means the sole purpose for your decisions and choices in life are coming from a place of duality, separateness and are self centered. While it's important to put the wants, needs and desires of ourselves first through self love and self care, when it comes to a broad perspective, can we be community minded?

The story I am sharing is how my own 'awakening' unfolded. There were several years where I was searching and recreating my life. I began trusting my intuition more and more. I was moving from place to place and I was finding out who I was from many different perspectives.

CHAPTER 2

Yoga. It's Not About the Pose

I was in the middle of a divorce when I started noticing something inside. It was my Higher Self, 'Source' (also known as my intuition), and it was communicating with me. I was familiar with the word, "source" through my introduction to the teachings of Abraham-Hicks but was not completely familiar with their teachings. Over time, I found the teachings of Abraham-Hicks resonated with me and my life.

After several years of living the life I had created, I was finding my way teaching classes and working with clients in various yoga and Pilates studios in Southern California. I found myself becoming more and more tuned in to my authentic self. I had been exploring alternative healing modalities and was beginning to break through some of the patterns and programs from my early childhood, as well as childhood trauma. It was a time in my life where I learned to just 'go within'. I was beginning to trust my intuition more and more and after a while, I learned how to listen and navigate from that place, my Higher Self.

What I realized was that I had been tuned in to my intuition most of my life. I, like most children, started communicating with my Higher Self, my Angels and Guides at an early age. It came clear to me that frequent suppressive parenting was responsible for creating doubt in my mind. This effected my ability to trust myself and it effected my self esteem. I can actually remember a time where I began to doubt myself and my intuition. It's important to know that our parenting also comes through those who are not our parents. Parenting shows up in our lives through siblings and babysitters, as well as teachers and others.

It was after those years of various techniques used to unearth the layers of programming and 'dogma' I received growing up, I began to hear my intuition regularly, and more clearly. What I heard led me to the unfolding of what my book, *The Shift, Awakening Into This Aquarian Age*, is about.

We all have the same inner guidance system. It is our Source or our Intuition. As we grow up and evolve in our lives there is the potential to tune out or ignore our inner guidance, our intuition. This can happen in part, through programmed parenting as well as particular obstacles and barriers we may have. It is neither good or bad, right or wrong, but it is the inheritance of the ancestry from which we have come. If the parenting we received as children, or the guidance we receive as teens and young adults, does not reflect evolution and forward movement into a changing world, we can be programmed to live the same lives and make the same mistakes as our parents… our ancestry.

When we lose the ability to hear or trust our intuition it can lead to imbalance and dis-ease. Author, Healer Louise Hay has mentioned numerous times, how cancer is caused by the deep buried emotions of anger.

When we are aligned with our inner guidance and are hearing what our intuition is telling us, we will find ourselves in a place of balance and ease. We won't be suffering from illness and maladies that man has created and labeled.

When we are in alignment we are joyous and fulfilled. And, chances are we are doing what we came into this lifetime to do or we are on path to discovering just what we have come to do. There is no mistake, when we are doing what we have incarnated into our bodies to do we are, indeed, on top of the world! All is well and all is right from within. We are finding no negative with anything within our lives. Our life is in alignment with who we are, what we came here to do and what we want in our lives.

It is when we decide to start thinking for ourselves and connect to our 'Higher Self', our intuition, that we will become aligned. We know we have moved into alignment when things start to fall in to place as to what we want in our lives. Even if we are not crystal clear on what we want at the time, we are moving into alignment simply by living and doing what shows up in front of us. We are being 'pulsed' by that which we are attracting into our lives via the Law of Attraction.

This is how to live your life as a *'Unified Being'*. It is living your Divinity. If you are living your Divinity you are not only doing what you came into this lifetime to do but you are moving forward into that which lights you up. And, that is your *Soul's Life Purpose!*

As we go about our lives we will shift from being in and out of alignment. This is all part of the *dance* we have signed up for in this 'Earth School' we are attending. It is a piece to the greater whole of the reason we have incarnated into our bodies. We are wanting to experience contrast and learn particular lessons to become more evolved spiritual beings and more loving spiritual beings. And yes, Dear One, we are here to actually experience and **feel** Love, the human expression of Love!

CHAPTER 3

Big Change

After moving to Florida from California in 2010, I set out to recreate my life, myself, once again. Only this time, it was the role of a caregiver, a daughter looking after her mother.

From 2010 to her death in Year 2019, I was the predominant caregiver to my mother. It was through this experience of looking after my mother for 9 years, that I left myself.

I know now, in order to care for anyone, I must first care for and love myself.

During this major life transition, I found myself letting go of my own life, what I had incarnated into this lifetime to experience. I let go of my own need for work and resources, as every time I set out to claim any sort of independence and individuality, my mother would decline another level.

I had been in California since 1995. Though I had moved around a bit, I had a thriving Yoga and Pilates business and practice. I had relied on my own personal practice to give me the strength and wherewithal to carry a full schedule. Just prior to my departure, I had experienced several life changes that made 'leaving everything' a viable option. And, after hearing from several of my mother's friends that she was showing signs of cognitive impairment, when she invited me to leave California and move in with her in Florida, I accepted.

Letting go is an art form, a process and a decision. It's a decision to physically let go and allow for the process to occur throughout your Being on many different levels.

Letting go is a choice. It's a form of consciousness that allows for freedom and forward movement.

As one chooses to let go, the process begins. As I have learned, there are many different aspects to letting go. I believe it all depends upon what you are letting go of. What is being let go?

Through the many levels and variations within the actual process of letting go, it's important to identify with an intention. If there has been a death, letting go can evolve through the subconscious for many years.

Perhaps it's time to begin anew, the letting go process can be multi faceted. There are people, places and things one could let go of to allow for a new beginning. A new life can emerge and unfold as we let go of that which no longer serves us in this lifetime and perhaps, for some, in other lifetimes.

CHAPTER 4

Who Are You?

It's Okay to Be Unique!

From an early age I was told I was 'so sensitive'. I never really knew what my family and teachers were talking about. My whole family would tell me how sensitive I was. I didn't know anything different. I was just doing my best to move through one day to the next. It was who I was.

I remember my mother telling me the doctor wanted her to put me on a drug so I could take naps at preschool as there was a lot of energy moving through me as a child, growing up and as a young adult. I was immersed in Health and Fitness. From dance, volleyball, swimming, and athletics, I learned to channel my energy through activity and action. When I was in my 40's, I began to expand and explore my 'authentic self'. I opened to my gifts as a Reiki Healer and found how sensitive I truly was. I had been teaching Pilates, Yoga and Dance for years but this was different. The energy was so palpable, I really didn't get it at first. Wasn't everyone experiencing energy that way?

I started expanding my awareness through my practice and experiences with Reiki and found myself seeing clients for 'Reiki Energy Healing' sessions. It all just flowed and it came together with the other aspects of energy medicine that were coming forward to me at that time. Through the use of crystals, essential oils and flower essences, along with Reiki Energy Healing, I was able to transcend my own physical imbalances and pass along my experiential results to my clients. And it worked! There was one thing I found essential for optimal results and that one thing was my client needed to be open to receive the healing 'medicine' flowing through me and these natural, energetic tools from Gaia Mother Earth.

It was all so seamless, how my opening to these amazing gifts and 'knowingness' was guiding me forward to the next phase of my work, my life. I was being shown the path and direction that was introducing me to a new phase of my life. For the first time I was aware of My Soul's Life Purpose!

What is your 'Soul's Life Purpose', anyway?

It's what we incarnate into this lifetime, into each lifetime to do. It's our accomplishments and our goals throughout our lives and it shows up differently at different times in our lives.

For instance, have you ever had a burning desire to do something in particular? Something that is number one on your wish list, your bucket list or your things to do? Well, that is what your 'Soul's Life Purpose' is all about. You see your *'soul'* is YOU. But it's all of you. It's who you are from a broader perspective and it allows you to soar… to fly with the eagles, it connects you to that which Lights You Up! And, when you reach that or achieve the place within you that you are knowing - your Soul's *Life Purpose*, that which lights you up and is driving you through every minute of every day - then you know you have arrived. You are home! You are tapping into your Divinity, your Truth and you are moving forward.

It is from that place, you and your life will come into alignment. Not just you, though, things around you and things that allow you to move forward with *Grace* and *Ease*. This is truly living your Divinity.

After moving forward and healing through a traumatic life event, I realized I had arrived, once again. I have turned on and tuned in to my *gifts,* my God Gifts. These are the aspects of me that are evolving and coming up to the surface that I am meant to tap into at this time in my life.

It took me experiencing a traumatic event, a life altering event, that cracked me wide open to this aspect of me and my life. I had to be 'shaken up' to wake up and become aware that I was living a life that was completely out of alignment and wrong for me.

It is at this particular time that it's all happening because I have reached the phase of my life, past my prime, which is the 'Setting Sun' phase of the Human Life Experience. The beauty of this phase of life, when we are connected to our Higher Self, is that we are living our Divinity.

The 'Setting Sun' phase of life means we are on the downward slope of the large *bell curve* of our life experience. We have indeed, moved forward through the prime of our lives. As a female, moving into this phase of life puts me in a position to open to my innate gifts as a '*wisdom keeper*' or a crone (to put it in lay terms). This phase of the life experience is a gift in that it reveals my Truth. As I reveal my truth, it creates change. And it is this *change* that is happening now.... in my life and on the planet.

Embarking on a new life experience and journey at 60 years of age may seem like a big task, but when it is your Soul's Life Purpose, your Divinity, you are moving into alignment and everything around you will change and move into alignment to clear the path for your forward movement ... everything!

CHAPTER 5

The Highly Sensitive Child

As a Highly Sensitive Being there is an adaptability involved to living life. This involves awareness and self-care. There needs to be the ability to know and understand our authentic self. Chances are, if our parents are not Highly Sensitive they are not knowing how to equip us with the tools needed for us to understand 'who' we are and what our needs are from an early age.

Most Highly Sensitive children are inherently open hearted, trusting and naive. They may have big emotions as they are touched deeply by their own feelings and emotions, as well as those of other's. These children can also communicate differently from those less sensitive. Highly Sensitive children can be very sensitive to their environment, such as their room, their surroundings and even their clothing. Most of those gifted with animals are truly empathic Beings with a high level of sensitivity.

Before I realized I had different needs for navigating through life on a daily basis, I found myself being effected by life experiences differently than others. I was living and seeing life through a different lens than most, including my family and siblings. I found that I was living through a unique and different paradigm of sensory information, unlike those around me. I remember as a child in third grade, I was only able to wear certain fabrics and have my hair a particular way around my face and neck.

After reaching adulthood, I began to realize and understand how I was affected by people, Energy and events in my life. As science tells us, everything is Energy and to an Empathic person, that *Energy* is palpable.

I remember my sister telling me a story about a family trip she, her husband and her two children had taken. They were on a road trip and stopped at a motel to stay the night before journeying further on their adventure. After checking in, they went up to their room. Her son, who was in high school at the time, entered the room first. While in the doorway he stopped, turned and looked at them and said, "Oh no. I don't like the vibe of this place!" It was after that, I knew my instincts about my nephew being Highly Sensitive, were correct.

CHAPTER 6

Your Inner World

After years of being in the Health & Fitness Industry, I evolved into Healing Arts. I had always known Pilates from my dance background, but after moving to the San Francisco Bay Area, I was guided to expand my knowledge and get certified to teach Pilates on the apparatus.

Going through the extensive Pilates training was life altering. Not only was I being taught by a 2nd Generation teacher from Joseph Pilates, himself, but her style of teaching resonated with me in such a way - I was able to go deeper into my own practice. I became immersed in teaching Pilates throughout the Bay Area and when the Claremont Hotel and Resort expanded their offerings and opened a Pilates Studio, I was there!

It was like magic. The members and guests of the Club at the Claremont were one of a kind. They were unique in that they had a thirst to go inside and explore their 'inner world' - their 'stuff'. They wanted to heal themselves. With that opportunity offered to me client after client, I had my 'Aha' moment with regard to my relationship with Pilates Training and what kind of Instructor I was. What my students were teaching me was the journey to self discovery and self realization was attainable through various Pilates exercises and breathing techniques. After hearing about their breakthroughs, I soon discovered my own path to my 'inner world', my Authentic Self.

It was during this time I was attracted to spending what little time I had, immersed in my yoga practice. I found it was the balancing ingredient in my life that allowed me to sort through the minutiae of details and stuff that flowed into my world every day. I was able to find 'stillness' through yoga and it was in part, due to my teacher. Through that stillness, I came to hear my mind and what it was creating through thought. Though I wasn't quite a 'master' of my thoughts at the time, I knew I was on the right path. And that path was a path to a relationship with myself.

As a Highly Sensitive and Empathic Adult, I have experienced the challenges of being Highly Sensitive and I have now experienced the **Gifts** of being Highly Sensitive. I know if I choose to, I can open up to a whole big, big world of energy! We all can. However, it is in the *practice* and the *journey* to understanding who I truly am and why I am here that has led me to find balance and stability in my life.

I know to stay grounded, clear and centered in my heart and to connect with my true authentic self, my daily practice, my **Sadhana,** needs to be a cornerstone of my daily life experience. It is through my practice that I stay in communication and in touch with who I truly am and what I want, need and desire in this lifetime. This is the path of a Highly Sensitive Being. This is the story of an Empath.

Printed in the United States
by Baker & Taylor Publisher Services